Kalahari Blues

Kalahari Blues

and other plays

Miriam Gallagher

Cover Design by Gerhardt Gallagher

ISBN   0-9538200-1-7
First published in 2006
Mirage
Dublin
Ireland

Contents

About the Author

Miriam Gallagher, Irish playwright, novelist & screenwriter, studied Drama in London (LAMDA). Her work, staged & screened in Ireland, London, Paris, USA & Canada with Irish, Dutch, Finnish and Russian translations, is included in the *Field Day Anthology of Irish Writing* and profiled in *Irish Women Writers: An A-Z Guide* (Geenwood Press,CT, USA, 2006)

This volume follows her book of plays: *Fancy Footwork* (Soc. Irish Playwrights, 1997, 2nd Ed) which includes plays produced between 1983 and 1997.

She has published a novel, *Song for Salamander*, (Trafford 2004) and short stories in anthologies of Irish Writing. Non fiction includes *Let's Help Our Children Talk* (O'Brien Press 1977) and essays commissioned by *The Irish Times,* arts, literary, film & educational journals. Rté has broadcast her radio plays, her essays on *Sunday Miscellany,* and her film *Gypsies,* screened in New York's Lincoln Center & San Francisco.

Miriam has received Arts Council & European Script Fund Awards for her feature length screenplay *Girls in Silk Kimonos* (celebrating the Gore Booth sisters) EU Theatre Award, a Writer's Exchange to Finland & MHA (Mental Health Assoc) Tv Script Award. She presented work at the 4th and 5th International

Women's Playwrights Conferences in Galway & Athens, and recently in Marseille at Semaine Mondiale des Auteurs Vivants de Théatre 2006.

She has worked in professional, prison & community Theatre. Commissions include *The Ring of Mont de Balison*,(Ranelagh Millennium Project) *Kalahari Blues* (Galloglass Theatre Co) which toured nationwide; *The Gold of Tradaree* (Clare Arts Award) *The Mighty Oak of Riverwood* (Betty Ann Norton Theatre School 40 years celebration) performed at the Gate Theatre; *Blue Heaven* (Red Kettle Theatre Co.) and *Fancy Footwork* (Dublin Theatre Festival) which was performed by Mountjoy prisoners at Focus Theatre, Dublin: a unique occasion, being the only time in the history of the State that prisoners were released to perform in a professional theatre.

A member of Irish PEN, Miriam has served on its committee and as vice president. She has also served on the Irish Writers Union committee, the council of the Society of Irish Playwrights, as a judge for the O.Z. Whitehead Play Competition and on the Awards Panel for Arts & Disability Forum.

She has given scriptwriting courses at Rté Training unit, An Creagan Arts Centre, schools, colleges, prisons and arts centres. She has been a guest lecturer at universities in Dublin, New York, Boston & Pretoria.

Her mss are in the National Library and film work in the Irish Film Archive.

Kalahari Blues

Original Production

Kalahari Blues was first performed by Galloglass Theatre Co. on 15th October 2001 at the Church of Ireland Parochial Hall, Clonmel, Co. Tipperary with the following:

LIAM	Ciarán Taylor
AFRIC	Una Mc Nulty
JASON	John Anthony Murphy
SAM	Anne-Marie McAuley
Director	Theresia Guschlbauer
Designer	Anna Fleischle
Composer	Denis Clohessy
Lighting	Paul Denby
Stage Manager	Katherine Mahony
Production Manager	David Teevan
Asst Stage Manager	Tríona Ward
Wardrobe Coordinator	Ann O' Mahony
Lighting operator	Ian Wilford
Set construction	Take Biijlsma & Tony Glavin

Characters & Setting

LIAM, *untidy, aspiring writer, passionate about the desert*

AFRIC, *sculptor, frail but steel- like in practical matters*

JASON, *entrepreneur/web designer, excitable, garrulous*

SAM, *classy, enigmatic,androgynouslike business icon*

The action takes place in a decaying sitting room of an old house, in an Irish town in the late 1990s.

Kalahari Blues was commissioned by Galloglass Theatre Co. for 2001 National Tour. Together with Johann Nestroy's *Previous Relations* & Sean O'Casey's *Bedtime Story* it toured under the title 'A Prime Location.'

(PLAY opens with MUSIC. LIGHTS fade up on decaying sittingroom of an old town house.The room is lit by a bare bulb & sparsely furnished: An armchair, an old picture, an empty vase, two upright chairs. At a table, LIAM, a dishevelled would-be-author, is writing. He pauses, frowns, screws up the page, hurls it Offstage He starts another page, sighs loudly, and screwing it up, hurls it Offstage. He rises and paces, pauses expectantly then shakes his head, resumes pacing, then stops, his face lighting up as if struck by inspiration. He dashes to the table, and writes feverishly)

LIAM.   *(writing)* Oh now, Liam me boyo, you're on the pig's back *(laughs)* James Joyce watch out! *(writes, then stops at the sound of a knock on the door, sighs)* That'll be the Mormons *(resumes writing, stops during persistent knocking on the door)* Go and save someone else!

(Another knock. Liam opens the door, stares at AFRIC with her belongings)

LIAM.   *(resigned)* Yes?

AFRIC.   *(smiles sweetly)* This is Woodbine House?

LIAM.   It is. But ...

AFRIC.   Can I come in?

LIAM.   No *(trying to close the door)* Thanks for calling

(AFRIC brushes past him, dumping her things SC.)

LIAM.   *(affronted)* You have no right to . . .

AFRIC.   *(looking around)* Not very inspiring is it? *(sniffs)* But dry *(shivers)* Ugh! I wouldn't fancy living in the basement and as for those stairs! *(shaking his hand)* I'm Afric. And you must be . . .?

LIAM.   *(taken aback)* Liam *(irritated)* Listen here

AFRIC.   *(starting to unpack)* I'll leave my things here for the moment

LIAM.   You will not. Off you go. I have work to do

AFRIC.   So have I. That's why I'm here

LIAM.   *(pauses)* You're not from a publisher are you?

AFRIC.   What?

LIAM.   *(embarrassed)* I'm only on the first chapter but *(whispers)* I think I have the plot *(showing off)* Once I get going, it'll write itself

AFRIC.   *(amused)* No. I'm not a publisher

LIAM.   *(disappointed)* Ah!

AFRIC.   I'm a sculptor

LIAM.   *(impressed)* Oh! is that so now?

AFRIC.   Yes. That's why Jason picked me *(pokes in her things)*

LIAM.   Who's Jason?

AFRIC.   Didn't he tell you I was coming? *(as he shakes his head)* Typical nerd behaviour

LIAM.   *(inspecting her things)* Are they your . . .?

AFRIC.   Just materials. I need somewhere to work

LIAM.   There's an empty room upstairs

AFRIC.   But is it dry?

LIAM.   *(laughs)* As dry as you'll get

AFRIC.   *(glancing around)* How long are you here?

LIAM.   A few months. Mind you the cold was fierce during the winter

AFRIC.   Why did you come?

LIAM.   *(hesitates)* That's a long story

AFRIC.   Ah! But if I'm moving in we might as well get to know each other

LIAM.   *(sizing her up)* A drink?

AFRIC.   Thanks (*sits in armchair*)

(*He fills two glasses. She smiles, takes glass. They drink*)

AFRIC.   Well?

LIAM.   (*sighs*) I got thrown out of the last place (*as she goes to speak*) And don't ask me why

AFRIC.   Was it the rent?

LIAM.   (*offended*) Nothing like that

AFRIC.   (*pauses*) Did you do something awful?

LIAM.   I'm not saying

AFRIC.   Go on

LIAM.   (*embarrassed*) No

AFRIC.   (*crosses her heart*) Cross my heart. I won't tell a soul

LIAM.   (*reluctant*) She thought I fancied her

AFRIC.   Who?

LIAM.   The landlady

AFRIC.   (*amused*) And did you?

LIAM.   God no but she was after me like a bullet.

LIAM.   Wouldn't leave me alone. And then things got out of hand with her cornering me in the bedroom while her husband was out on the night shift (*shudders*) I had to get away

(*They laugh*)

AFRIC.   Listen, I hope we'll be friends

LIAM.   (*goes to table, sits, then relieved*) Just as well you're not a publisher. I'm not really ready yet for the bookshops

AFRIC.   What are you writing?

LIAM.   (*diffident*) It's private. You know

AFRIC.   Sure. Must get boring everyone asking you what you're writing

LIAM.   (*clears throat*) This is my first...book

AFRIC.   Why did you decide to write it?

LIAM.   Ah! I just had to. It's hard to explain

AFRIC.   (*curious*) Is it about yourself?

LIAM.   (*awkward*) Kinda

AFRIC.   (*eager*) An autobiography

LIAM.   (*modest*) Well I wouldn't say that exactly

AFRIC.   What's it called?

LIAM.   You'll laugh if I tell you

AFRIC.   No I won't

LIAM.   Sure?

AFRIC.   Try me

LIAM.   *(hesitates, then proudly)* Kalahari Blues

AFRIC.   *(laughs)* Wow!

LIAM.   I knew you'd laugh

AFRIC.   No, it sounds great

LIAM.   Really?

AFRIC.   Yeh. Would you read a bit for me?

LIAM.   *(inwardly pleased)* Ah, I don't know

AFRIC.   Go on. And I can show you some of my work *(pauses)* Listen, who knows I might even do a bust of you

LIAM.   *(impressed)* Really? *(she nods)* Well all right so *(takes up a page, clears throat, reads to her encouraging nods)* Liam knew he was different from other fisherman. In his heart he longed to answer the call of the desert. So, one dark, starry night, he took up his

LIAM.   trumpet and played, Kalahari Blues.

AFRIC.   Wow! (*as he hesitates*) Go on

LIAM.   He played every night of his life until one day---

(*At the sound of jaunty whistling outside the door, Liam stops reading and replaces his page on the table. They both stare as ENTER JASON breezily, entrepreneur with slick briefcase*)

JASON.   (*shaking hands*) Hello Afric, Liam. Good to see you two already know each other

LIAM.   And you are . . .?

JASON.   Jason, your webmaster (*puts case on table, opens it*) Now, let's get hooked up (*noting Liam's surprise*) Ooh! but do I see surprise in someone's eyes?

LIAM.   You can say that again

JASON.   Alrighty. I'll run through the basics (*eager*) Woodbine House is now owned by dreamsitedotcom (*pauses for effect*) Just imagine! This old place, virtually falling down around our ears, has a virtual future. All thanks to dreamsite

LIAM.   (*doubtful*) How?

JASON.   (*grins*) By becoming a virtual dreamsite and helping people realise their dreams.

LIAM.   *(bewildered)* What d'you mean?

JASON.   Dreamsite is where we drop pretences and become ourselves *(grins)* by making all the right moves. That's it in a nutshell. Alrighty? From now on our "email address" is *(makes 'quotes' with fingers)* "rightmove@dreamsitedotcom". Now *(giving leaflets)* Make yourselves at home

LIAM.   *(under his breath)* I thought I was at home

JASON.   *(wags finger)* Ah-ah! Not in that sense *(grins)* Remember Woodbine House is now a home for other people's dreams

(Afric and Liam exchange puzzled glances as ENTER SAM, dead cool, smartly dressed in black with black and silver accessories. She carries a slick computer case)

JASON.   Sam *(air kisses Sam's cheek)*

SAM.   Jason *(offering the other cheek for air kissing)*

JASON.   This is Sam "Top Dog" at dreamsite

(Liam & Afric nod awkwardly at Sam,who smiles frostily)

SAM.   What this town needs is a progressive arts and business centre, a virtual site *(pauses)* manned by artists and business types

JASON.   *(eager)* Artists of course live rent free *(pauses slightly)* And all expenses paid. Alrighty?

LIAM. *(impressed)* Oh I see *(glances at Afric)* Well that's different

JASON. So different it'll change the image of this neighbourhood forever *(intense)* Like dreamsitedot com has done for other places before

SAM. *(glares at Jason)* Yes *(opens case)* Now for the plans

(Sam pins up plans for the site. Afric & Liam look at plans while Jason inspects gizmo from her case)

AFRIC. But what happens if Boomtime doesn't last and all the dotcoms collapse?

JASON. *(peals of laughter)* As if! Glorious Child, do you have imagination! *(to Sam)* No wonder she's an artist *(to Afric)* Seriously, you're as safe as houses with dreamsitedotcom.

SAM. *(looks at furnishings with distaste)* Ugh! People do we need to smarten up! Jason, we're a website on the super-highway, not a hostel for down & outs *(indicates fireplace & items)* That has to go. And that. And that

JASON. Of course *(puts gizmo back in case)*

LIAM. *(suspicious)* What do we have to do?

SAM. *(enigmatic)* Answer people's needs.

JASON. *(eager)* When they email us at "rightmove@ dreamsitedotcom" *(indicates quotation marks with fingers)* we give them what they want.

LIAM. But how does it work?

SAM. *(to Jason after giving Liam a pitying glance)* Show them

JASON. Alrighty

SAM. Let's go

(Blackout. MUSIC in b/g to mechanistic Sounds of Cyberspace. LIGHTS flicker, then as MUSIC becomes jazzy, LIGHTS change. The fireplace is gone (or blacked out) Smart office chairs. Laptop & gadgets on desk. Flowcharts depicting www.dreamsite.com are attached to walls or office type furniture. Actors have backs to audience and wear black jackets. Jazzy MUSIC as Actors take sunglasses from pockets, hold them aloft, then put them on. ALL turn in unison, dance briefly and end with a flourish facing out front)

JASON. We're virtually there

LIAM. Where?

JASON. *(regarding 'giant computer monitor' out front)* Cyberspace

LIAM. *(staring)* But is it real?

SAM.   (*enigmatic*) What you see is what you get

AFRIC.   Yeh but (*giggles. Sam's glare silences her*) O.K. No sweat.

(*Computer activity: beeps and clicks./ buttons flashing.All regard 'screen' out front*)

JASON.   Our first message (*to Liam*) Go on! JASON. (*points to laptop on desk*) Read it

LIAM.   (*reads*) I dream of the perfect mate. How can I join Cybermates?

SAM.   Simply look up our Link page

JASON. And click onto (*intense*) friendsforever@ bunnyclubdotcom

AFRIC.   Here's more (*hands Emails to Liam*)

LIAM.   (*reading*)   I want to ride in the Grand National and win. Can you give me my dream?

JASON.   (*urgent*) That's what we're here for

(*Jason pins up Email. Afric & Liam exchange amused looks. Sam gives a stony stare*)

JASON.   (*to Liam*) Go on

LIAM.   (*reading*) I dream of climbing Mount Everest

SAM.   Delete

LIAM.   Hey! this is a dreamsite. Don't they get their dreams?

SAM.   (*looks at watch*) Playtime (*pulls Jason by his tie*)

JASON.   Already? (*get closer*) Alrighty (*gets cosy*) Mm

(*They EXIT. Afric shrugs, joins Liam with sorting emails*)

LIAM.   (*to Afric*) If you ask me the whole thing is a disaster

AFRIC.   Yeh but rent free

LIAM.   They're both weirdos with their cyber this and cyber that. Dotcom how are you! (*laughs*) Listen to this (*reading*) Cyberspy. Discover anything about anyone with clickable hyperlinks and no typing in Internet addresses. Locate a past lover who broke your heart. Send anonymous email completely untraceable! Get information on an ex-spouse. Dig up old skeletons and win in court. Discover what dirty secrets your mysterious neighbours are hiding. Learn about people you work with

AFRIC.   Hm. Maybe we could use dreamsite for our own ends

LIAM.   But how?

AFRIC.   (*smiling*) I'm working on it

(Sam and Jason ENTER, patting hair into place etc.)

SAM.   *(glances at watch)* Time's up

JASON.   *(still cosy)*   Mmmm *(being pushed away)* Alrighty

(Computer sounds, flashing lights. Emails arrive)

LIAM.   *(reading)* I want to make the right move

SAM.   Just the upwardly mobile type we need at dreamsite

JASON.   *(mutters)* You should know

SAM.   *(to Jason)*   And what's that supposed to mean?

JASON.   Nothing

(An embarrassed silence. Sam sits on chair DSR.)

LIAM.   Will I go on?

SAM.   What?

AFRIC.   With the dreams

SAM.   *(snaps)* Yes

JASON.   *(smooth)* After all that's why we're here

LIAM. *(reading)* I'm looking for a dream house in a prime location. Must have 20 bedrooms, swimming pool, sauna, and skating rink

SAM. Respond

LIAM. But how can we produce all that?

SAM. We virtually can *(looks around)* Where are the new printers? Still outside in the car? *(to Jason, giving him car keys)* Well, get them *(to Liam)* Remember business interests are paying for this enterprise. So get busy

JASON. Alrighty *(beckons Liam)*

(THEY EXIT)

SAM. *(smooth)* There's virtually no end to virtual reality

AFRIC. Yeh but *(pauses)* what's in it for me?

SAM. You could use the web to sell your work

AFRIC. Really?

SAM. *(enigmatic)* I could help you

AFRIC. With my career?

SAM. Honey, trust me

AFRIC. (*backs off as Sam moves nearer*) I don't think so

(*Jason and Liam return with boxes. Sam indicates where to put them, holds out hand for car keys*)

JASON.   (*gives keys, frowns*) Did you take my accounts spreadsheets?

SAM.   No. (*smooth*) Why would I do that?

JASON.   (*searching*) Where's my calculator?

SAM.   Over there

(*Jason grabs calculator. As mobile phone rings, hesitates, suddenly switches it off*)

SAM.   Is anything wrong?

JASON.   (*snaps*) No. Why should there be? (*feverishy uses calaclator, frowns*)

AFRIC.   (*to Liam*) I'm going to sell my work on the Internet

LIAM.   How?

AFRIC.   (*smiling*) I'm working on it

(*Computer sounds. Email arrives*)

AFRIC.   (*reading*)   I am all alone. Can I join Cybermates?

SAM.   Respond

AFRIC.   What'll I say?

JASON.   Use your imagination, Honey.

AFRIC.   But it could be from an axe murderer

SAM.   It could (*looks at Jason,then points to Liam*)
Respond!

JASON.   Like a real Cybermate

LIAM.   What? Me?

SAM.   Give the lady what she wants

LIAM.   How do we know it's from a woman?

JASON.   We don't (*pauses*) Go on

LIAM.   (*reading*) Is the light off? (*mystified*) Are you
ready to xxxxxxx?

JASON.   Could be a virus

LIAM.   I don't want to catch anything

SAM.   You're quite safe at dreamsite

JASON.   (*glancing at Afric*) On the other hand those
xxxxxxx could be kisses

30

AFRIC.   (*under her breath*) You should know

JASON.   Go on

LIAM.   (*reading with growing distaste*) Why don't you slip into something satiny and we can xxxxxxx. What's that supposed to mean?

SAM.   Whatever the client wants it to mean

LIAM.   (*as meaning dawns*) Listen, I'm not a gigolo

SAM.   Don't be ridiculous

LIAM.   (*blustering*) Anyway I eh don't wear satin

SAM.   Does anyone? (*glances at Afric who looks away*)

JASON.   *to Liam*) Would you disappoint a lonely person?

AFRIC.   An axe murderer

JASON.   (*smooth*) Someone with real needs

SAM.   Virtually one of us.

JASON.   We must do all we can to help people

AFRIC.   Save them from themselves

JASON.   It's the least we can do

SAM.   For our fellow human beings

JASON.   For anyone

AFRIC.   Even an axe murderer

JASON.   If we do our best then

SAM & JASON.   (*smiling*) so should you

(*Computer noises. Email arrives*)

AFRIC   (*reading*) I want to make the right move

SAM.   Good. Another upwardly mobile type

AFRIC   (*reading*) You promised me a dream
mansion with fifty five bedrooms, a golf course, a lake
and a yacht if I sent a deposit of three million Euros.
But did I get what I asked for? (*pauses surprised, then
reading*) If you don't satisfy me I'll join 'Cybermates
Anon' (*presses buttons*)

JASON.   (*upset, stares out front at 'giant computer
monitor'*) No! It's Cyberspy!

SAM.   (*trying to keep cool*) Calm down

JASON.   (*gesticulating at' Cyberspy'*) Don't think you
can get away with this.

SAM.   Jason, control yourself

JASON.   Leave me alone *(gets more agitated)*

SAM.   You know what happened before

JASON.   But this is different to before

SAM.   That's what you said the last time

(Strange grinding computer noises)

JASON.   He's making the same noises again *(whispers)* but I'm ready this time *(looking out front at 'Big Screen')* You sicken me. Think you can infect me do you? *(hisses)* Well, I'll give you bugs *(attacking machines, karate style)* Take that. And that *(removes jacket, then with false bravado to 'Big Screen')* Come outside and fight like a real man

(Jason gives a last karate chop at machines on desk, EXITS. Computer sounds fizzle out)

SAM.   *(shouts after Jason)* You've virtually ruined everything *(turns to Afric)* What are you grinning at?

(Sam seizes her briefcase and storms out)

AFRIC.   Whew!

LIAM.   What was that all about?

AFRIC.   *(with a knowing look)* Remember Cyberspy?

LIAM.   *(as meaning dawns)* You mean you traced

LIAM.   "our friend" through the Internet?

AFRIC.   (*nods*) Ah ha! (*smiles*) One of its many uses

LIAM.   Spying?

AFRIC.   As if I would!

LIAM.   (*laughs then glances at door*) D'you think they're coming back?

AFRIC.   Dunno

LIAM.   (*gauche*) Well, I suppose that just leaves the two of us

AFRIC.   Alone in dreamsite!

LIAM.   Yeh

AFRIC.   Strangers in paradise!

(*Afric playfully pirouettes, then sits in armchair DSR.*)

LIAM.   Yeh but (*coughs*) Where do we go now?

AFRIC.   (*jokes*) We could join Cybermates

LIAM.   (*laughs*) And become like them? No fear

AFRIC.   (*with a knowing look*) What's wrong with making Cyberspace work for us?

LIAM.   How?

AFRIC.   We could run dreamsitedotcom ourselves

LIAM.   *(shudders)* Oh, I'm not cut out for all that cyber stuff

AFRIC.   *(mock serious)* It's the way of the future

LIAM.   Ah! You can keep it

AFRIC.   Listen, if we got the computer fixed you could use it for your work

LIAM.   I can't use a computer

AFRIC.   But I could teach you

LIAM.   Ah! I think I'd prefer the old pen *(takes laptop USL.)*

AFRIC.   *(pauses)* We could always make this place our dreamsite

LIAM.   That depends

AFRIC.   On what?

LIAM.   How we get on

AFRIC.   That's not going to be a problem is it ?

LIAM.   But is the place big enough for two?

AFRIC.   Mmm. I'll explore the rest of the house.
What about the room upstairs?

LIAM.   *(shrugs)* You're welcome to it

AFRIC.   Why? Is it damp?

LIAM.   Much like the rest of the place

AFRIC.   That's not saying much

LIAM.   Suit yourself *(sits at table with pen and paper)*

AFRIC.   I suppose you got the only dry room in
the house

LIAM.   *(smiles)* If you get lonely you can always
come down and see me

AFRIC.   *(laughing)* You'd be so lucky

(AFRIC EXITS with her things)

LIAM.   *(laughs, then takes out pages, concentrates, rises,
then reads, as he paces)* All through that long, dark,
starry night, Liam played his trumpet *(looks up,
pleased, then reads)* At daybreak, the fishermen,
returning with boatfuls of fish, could hear the Atlantic
rollers crashing against the shore *(pauses for effect)* and
the lone cry of a seagull *(looks up, pleased)* Mmm. Nice
ring to that Liam *(reading)* They paid no heed to the
figure on the cliffs playing his heart out *(pauses)* or to
his music *(goes to table, takes pen, ponders, then writes)*

LIAM.   But, as Liam played on *(pauses)* the sound was wafted on the wind *(his face lights up)* all the way to Africa *(pauses)* And, in the Kalahari desert, tribesmen, resting on their spears *(looking up)* pricked up their ears *(pauses)* and listened

(SPOT on African Mask on chair or in fireplace winking briefly (and/or possibly onto silhouette of Tribesmen holding spears / or desert skyline -projected onto back wall - MUSIC drifts in as LGHTS FADE)

(END OF PLAY)

The Mighty Oak
of Riverwood

Original Production

The Mighty Oak of Riverwood was first
performed at the Gate Theatre, Dublin & the
Crypt, Dublin Castle, April 2001 by
Students of Betty Ann Norton Theatre School

Directed by . . . . Hilary Cahill.

*The play was commissioned to celebrate 40 yrs of
The Betty Ann Norton Theatre School*

Characters & Setting

MIGHTY OAK
WIND
VOICES & OAK LEAVES, BRANCHES, ROOTS
WISE WOMAN of the WOOD
BRID BADGER
BREFFNI BADGER
OISIN OWL
FIACRA DEER
FERDIA FOX
ROISIN RABBIT
GRAINNE WREN
MALACHI ROBIN
FISH
MAYOR
ALDERMEN

The action of the play takes place in Riverwood Forest with one scene (downstage) in the Mayor's office.

N.B. (Gaelic) Dáire Mhór = Mighty Oak
            Maith thú! = All Hail!

———————————

(PLAY opens with MUSIC. WOODLAND CREATURES gather in the Forest)

VOICES Dáire Mhór

VOICES. Maith thú!

VOICES. All hail!

VOICES. Mighty Oak of Riverwood!

VOICES. King of the Forest

(MUSIC.ALL Dance around the MIGHTY OAK. During DANCE, BRID BADGER ENTERS, secretly pins a Notice to a tree. As DANCE ends MUSIC FADES)

OISIN OWL. *(Sees notice)* What's this *(excited)* Ooh! An invitation

FERDIA FOX. Who's it from?

OISIN OWL. Brid Badger *(reading)* All woodland creatures are asked to a party with the River animals

VOICES. Mmm a party!

VOICES. Can we go?

OISIN OWL. Yes

VOICES. And us?

OISIN OWL.   (*laughs*) Yes. It says All woodland creatures (*pauses*) Well what are we waiting for? Let's get ready.

(*EXEUNT..MIGHTY OAK coughs, shakes its branches*)

MIGHTY OAK.   I don't feel well. Something is wrong. I can feel it in my leaves

OAK LEAVES.   We are the leaves of the Mighty Oak

OAK LEAVES.   When rain falls we spread a roof over the floor of the Forest

OAK LEAVES.   In our cooling shade Deer lie down to rest

(*ENTER BRID BADGER with basket of herbs and large Book entitled Special Badger Recipes.She sits on a toadstool and opens book*)

BRID BADGER.   Now for my special recipe (*reading*) Delicious Party Drink: Gather a handful of nettles, wild herbs and rose hips. Wash thoroughly. Then cover with water and leave to settle. Taste before serving. Note: Make sure you use clean water

(*ENTER WISE WOMAN of the WOOD, gathering herbs*)

BRID BADGER.   Wise Woman, I'm going to make a delicious party drink

44

WISE WOMAN of the WOOD.   That's nice (*comes over to look at book*) Mmm. All your badger recipes are special. But make sure the water is clean

BRID BADGER.   (*offended*) Of course

(*BRID BADGER EXITS*)

WISE WOMAN of the WOOD.   Now I've offended her (*sighs*) Oh dear!   And Badgers are such clean animals

MIGHTY OAK.   (*coughing*) I am sick

WISE WOMAN of the WOOD.   (*startled*) Dáire Mhór, Mighty Oak, what is the matter?

MIGHTY OAK.   I don't know. But something is not right. I can feel it in my leaves

WISE WOMAN of the WOOD.   I'll make you a nice healing drink with these herbs. Then you'll soon feel better

(*SHE gathers herbs. ENTER BREFFNI BADGER running, bumps into WISE WOMAN who drops herbs*)

WISE WOMAN of the WOOD.   Whoops!

BREFFNI BADGER.   Sorry!

WISE WOMAN of the WOOD.   Tck! Tck!Now look what you've done

BREFFNI BADGER.   I'll pick them up for you

WISE WOMAN of the WOOD.   (*sighs*) There's no point. I must have fresh herbs that are picked at twilight when the dew falls

BREFFNI BADGER.   I really am sorry

WISE WOMAN of the WOOD.   And I can't use herbs that have fallen on the ground

BREFFNI BADGER.   I'm very very very very sorry

WISE WOMAN of the WOOD.   Oh never mind. Off you go now and help Bríd with the party

(*EXIT BREFFNI BADGER*)

WISE WOMAN of the WOOD.   That healing drink will have to wait for a moment

MIGHTY OAK.   (*moans*) I am not well (*coughs*) I can feel it in my branches

OAK BRANCHES.   We are the branches of the Mighty Oak

OAK BRANCHES.   Birds nest in our lofty canopy

OAK BRANCHES.   When storms rage, we stand tall and strong, bending with the wind and never breaking

MIGHTY OAK.   (*coughs*) But I am sick

WISE WOMAN of the WOOD.   Dáire Mhór, King
of the Forest I will look after you

(*ENTER BREFFNI BADGER running*)

WISE WOMAN of the WOOD. Watch out!

BREFFNI BADGER.   (*gulps*) I almost forgot what I
came to tell you

WISE WOMAN of the WOOD.   (*resigned*) What is it?

BREFFNI BADGER.   A dream

WISE WOMAN of the WOOD. Ah! You'd better tell
me about it

(*THEY sit on toadstools SL. WIND Sounds*)

BREFFNI BADGER.   Last night a strong wind
started up. The noise was so loud I had to put my
paws over my ears to get to sleep (*pauses, then shivers*)
In my dream I went out into the wood where the
wind was dancing

(*MUSIC. LIGHTS Change. WIND ENTERS SR. ,dances*)

VOICES.   Sh! Shoo-oo-oo

WIND.   I fly through the wood with messages

VOICES.   Sh! Shoo-oo-oo

WIND.   I whisper into the ears of woodland creatures when snow is coming

VOICES.   Sh! Shoo-oo-oo

WIND.   I tickle the birds' feathers if rain is on its way

VOICES.   Sh! Shoo-oo-oo

WIND.   Sometimes the message I bring is too frightful for whispers. Then I must shout it out. If you can't bear the sound of it, watch while I dance *it (puts a finger to lips)* Sh!

(WIND DANCE. As MUSIC Fades, WIND EXITS. LIGHT change)

BREFFNI BADGER.   *(anxious)* what does it mean?

WISE WOMAN of the WOOD.   Mmm. You did well to tell me about your dream

BREFFNI BADGER.   Is it bad news?

WISE WOMAN of the WOOD.   Come with me and we will find out

(EXEUNT. DARKNESS. Owl hoots. then distant Noise of Bulldozers, heavy machinery etc. A PAUSE. MUSIC.

As LIGHTS fade up, BRID BADGER is fixing magical party lights as ALL ENTER)

BRID BADGER.   Hello. You're all welcome to the party. Malachi Robin & Grainne Wren, could you collect twigs for the fire?

(MALACHI ROBIN & GRAINNE WREN collect twigs)

BRID BADGER.   Is anyone hungry?

OISIN OWL.   Of course. Woodland creatures are always hungry

BRID BADGER.   Good. Breffni can you pass round the food ?

(ALL take biscuits and much happily. MALACHI ROBIN & GRAINNE WREN bring twigs which OISIN OWL makes into a fire)

OISIN OWL.   Now there's a nice fire to keep us all warm

BRID BADGER.   Thank you. And here's the party drink made from my special Badger recipe

(SHE pours out glasses of party drink and hands them around.Distant Sound of Bulldozers, heavy machinery etc.)

FERDIA FOX.   What was that?

BRID BADGER.   Listen!

(Louder Sound of Bulldozers, heavy machinery etc.)

MALACHI ROBIN.   I will fly over to the Ash trees
and find out what's happening

BREFFNI BADGER.   I'll keep watch from behind
that clump of hazel bushes

(BREFFNI BADGER & MALACHI ROBIN EXIT)

BRID BADGER.   Now please pass round the
biscuits *(smiles)* Anyone for some of the party drink?

*(SHE fills mugs. GRAINNE WREN gulps her drink,
suddenly coughs)*

OISIN OWL.   Grainne Wren, that's what happens
if you gulp your drink too fast *(drinks from mug,
suddenly coughs)*

ROISIN RABBIT.   Hah! Is that so Oisin Owl? Has
yours gone down the wrong way?

*(General laughter. BRID keeps filling mugs. FERDIA
FOX gulps drink, gets a coughing fit and falls down. ALL
try to alert BRID who eventually notices Fox coughing)*

BRID BADGER.   Goodness me! What's this? A party
guest coughing. Why didn't you tell me?

ALL.   Oh yes we did

BRID BADGER.   Oh no you didn't

ALL.   Oh yes we did

BRID BADGER.   Oh no you (*breaks off*) well anyway it's probably nothing

(*BRID claps FERDIA FOX on the back. He coughs up a plastic bottle top*)

BRID BADGER.   (*displays bottle top*) Gracious me! A plastic bottle top.Ferdia Fox could have choked on it. Now where did that come from?

ROISIN RABBIT.   From a picnic I'd say

BRID BADGER.   Mmm It's dangerous to leave that here. A creature could swallow it (*whispers*) or choke (*pauses, then relieved*) I'm glad Ferdia Fox is better now and can join in the fun

(*MUSIC.MIME Party Games. MUSIC Fades as ENTER MALACHI ROBIN*)

BRID BADGER.   Malachi Robin what's the news?

MALACHI ROBIN.   (*breathless*) I saw big machines at the river

OISIN OWL.   (*alarmed*) what?

MALACHI ROBIN.   They're digging away at the banks

OISIN OWL.   I'll fly to the river and see for myself

BRID BADGER.   Wait. Here is Breffni

(ENTER BREFFNI BADGER running)

BRID BADGER.   Well what is it?

BREFFNI BADGER.   I've never seen anything like it

BRID BADGER.   Like what?

BREFFNI BADGER.   I saw liquid from a big machine pouring in to the river

ROISIN RABBIT.   What about our fish?

BREFFNI BADGER.   Some of the minnows are floating in the river

(A general gasp. MALACHI ROBIN starts to cry)

OISIN OWL.   Crying won't help

(FIACRA DEER has a coughing fit, then faints. ALL try to revive him)

BRID BADGER.   Carry him to the Wise Woman of the Wood

(BREFFNI BADGER, OISIN OWL & HELPERS carry FIACRA DEER offstage. LIGHTS change. Sound of Bulldozers, heavy machinery. CREATURES shiver with fright)

BREFFNI BADGER.   We must do something
quickly

(ALL look at each other)

BRID BADGER.   I know! Let's send a message to
the Mayor

ALL.   Hear hear!

BRID BADGER.   Who will take the message?

(ALL look at BREFFNI)

BREFFNI BADGER.   I will

OISIN OWL.   Anyone else?

(BREFFNI BADGER EXITS. MUSIC. CROSSFADE
LIGHTS from Forest to DOWNSTAGE. MAYOR, hands
clasped behind his back, paces, watched anxiously by TWO
ALDERMEN)

ALDERMAN.   Lord Mayor, our plans for the city
are sure to work

MAYOR.   Mmmm

ALDERMAN.   The new factory at Riverwood will
make us rich

MAYOR.   Mmmm

ALDERMAN.   And with the city stretching all the way out to the countryside ------

(BUTLER ENTERS)

BUTLER.   Lord Mayor, Breffni Badger is outside with a message

MAYOR.   (impatient) show him in

(BUTLER ushers in BREFFNI BADGER & FISH, then bows & EXITS)

MAYOR.   Yes, what is it? I'm a very busy man

BREFFNI BADGER.   Lord Mayor, we need your help

MAYOR.   Speak up

BREFFNI BADGER. There's a disaster at Riverwood

MAYOR.   Well, what is it? Be quick

FISH.   A mysterious sickness (coughing) affecting the fish from the river

MAYOR.   (bored) Oh dear dear!

FISH.   And some of our minnows are (sobs)

MAYOR.   I can't take care of every little minnow

BREFFNI BADGER.   Lord Mayor, Fiacra Deer is very ill

MAYOR.   (*not impressed*) Really?

BREFFNI BADGER.   Too sick to come and see you himself. And that's not all

MAYOR   (*yawns*) Oh get on with it

BREFFNI BADGER   The Mighty Oak is sick

MAYOR   (*alarmed*) what?

(*ALDERMEN exhange worried glances*)

MAYOR.   Dáire Mhór? The Mighty Oak of Riverwood?

BADGER BREFFNI.   I'm afraid so

MAYOR.   The tree that gives shelter to all living creatures?

BREFFNI BADGER.   Yes

MAYOR.   I can't believe such a thing. When harsh winds blow, the branches of Ash and Hazel can be heard snapping but the lofty branches of the Mighty Oak bend without breaking

BADGER BREFFNI.   Not any more. The tree is groaning with pain

(A PAUSE)

MAYOR.   This is terrible news

BADGER BREFFNI.   Come with me and see for yourself

MAYOR.   I will. Lead the way

ALDERMAN.   What about our plans for the city?

MAYOR.   Hold all plans- for the moment

ALDERMAN.   But really Lord Mayor—

(MUSIC. EXEUNT. LIGHTS up in Forest. WISE WOMAN gives drink to FIACRA DEER, watched by WOODLAND CREATURES)

WISE WOMAN of the WOOD.   This may do the trick. Luckily I had some herbs put to one side for emergencies

(FIACRA DEER revives)

FIACRA DEER.   Did I miss the party?

OISIN OWL.   The party is over

WISE WOMAN of the WOOD.   The important thing is that you're well again

(ENTER MAYOR)

MAYOR.   What's this I hear about the Mighty Oak?

WISE WOMAN of the WOOD.   Come and see for yourself

(*MIGHTY OAK feebly shakes its leaves*)

MAYOR.   (*quiet*) Dáire Mhór, your branches are drooping

MIGHTY OAK.   My power is going from me

MAYOR.   This is terrible

(*MIGHTY OAK groans. MALACHI ROBIN cries*)

MIGHTY OAK.   (*weak*) I am suffocating. I can feel it in my roots

OAK ROOTS.   We are the roots of the mighty Oak

OAK ROOTS.   We need food and drink and space to grow

(*ALL exchange looks of alarm*)

MAYOR.   (*looking around*) We can't let the Oak die. Can we?

ALL.   No

MAYOR.   What are we to do at all? (*pauses*) Dáire Mhór, how can we save you?

MIGHTY OAK.   Bind my wounds. Let the sap flow again through my veins Give me space!

(A PAUSE)

MAYOR.   Mighty Oak, King of the Forest, we will move the factory away from Riverwood and you will be well again

(ALL cheer)

WISE WOMAN of the WOOD.   Lord Mayor, we can all help

ALL.   Yes

(GRAINNE WREN steps forward)

GRAINNE WREN.   Malachi Robin why don't we gather blue irises and make a ribbon to wind around the Mighty Oak?

WISE WOMAN of the WOOD.   That's a good idea It will show everyone that the bark and roots of the tree are beginning to heal

ALL.   Yes

WISE WOMAN of the WOOD.   Off you go then

(GRAINNE WREN& MALACHI ROBIN skip off)

WISE WOMAN of the WOOD.   Let us plant acorns from the Mighty Oak

OSIIN OWL.   So that Baby Oaks will sprout up where the acorns are planted

ALL. Yes

WISE WOMAN of the WOOD.   And the ribbon of blue irises will help to bind the wounds of the Mighty Oak (*puzzled*) but you know there's something puzzling me. I can't believe that anyone would deliberately set out to harm the King of the Forest and hurt the woodland creatures (*looks around*) Do you?

ALL. No

WISE WOMAN of the WOOD.   Then we must let everyone know how important it is to save the Mighty Oak

OISIN OWL.   Let's put up a few notices

ROISIN RABBIT.   Mind our Trees

FIACRA DEER.   Keep our Forests Clean

BRID & BREFFNI BADGER.   Save our Rivers

ALL.   Yes

(*LIGHTS change. ALL gather around the MIGHTY OAK*)

VOICES.   Dáire Mhór

VOICES.   Maith thú!

VOICES.   All hail!

VOICES.   Mighty Oak of Riverwood

VOICES.   King of the Forest!

(MUSIC. *MALACHI ROBIN & GRAINNE WREN dance on with a blue ribbon which ALL wind around the MIGHTY OAK in a DANCE)*

(*END OF PLAY*)

Midhir and the Firefly

Inspired by the Celtic tale of Midhir & Etain

Original Production

Midhir & the Firefly was first performed in 2000
at Martin Murphy High School, Hollister,
California, USA.

Directed by . . . . Jennifer Nestjoko.

Characters & Setting

BRESAL ETARLAIM, Narrator/ Druid / Shaman

MIDHIR, yellow haired with high good looks

ETAIN /FIREFLY, beautiful, hair like red gold after it is rubbed

KING EOCHAID, married to ETAIN,)

FUAMACH, dark haired, jealous, first wife to MIDHIR

ETARE, Fire Queen, wears half mask, dressed in red/gold

CHORUS. Druids

FIREFLIES, glowing, magical)

The play can be played on a bare stage.
Upstage Screen is suggested but not essential.

If actors double on parts; Chorus of two Druids.

Music

Celtic if possible (Flute, Whistle, Boireann)

Costume Suggestions

ETAIN wears flame coloured shimmering garments

FIREFLIES wear incandescent garments

STARS, black clad DANCERS holding twinkling lights)

FIRE QUEEN, gold crown, halfmask, cloak in shimmering Fire colours)

DRUIDS wear white robes

BRESAL wears white robes with a green sash

MIDHIR wears tunic, braided socks

KING EOCHAID, similar to MIDHIR,wears cloak

FUAMACH wears long red robe, hair dressed high on head.

(PLAY opens with MUSIC. ETARE, QUEEN of FIRE, dances with ETAIN & FIREFLIES. DANCERS move US. QUEEN & ETAIN disappear leaving FIREFLIES flickering (behind screen) CHORUS of DRUIDS (incl. BRESAL) enter from opposite sides, form semicircle facing out front)

ALL.   At dark of night

BRESAL.   the Queen of Fire

DRUID.   rides her chariot.

DRUID.   across the sky

BRESAL.   counting stars

(THREE DRUIDS move forward)

ALL.   She knows

DRUID.   every star by name,

BRESAL.   where they are,

DRUID.   how to find them.

DRUID.   when to bring them

DRUID.   from darkness

ALL.   into light

(TWO DRUIDS move forward)

ALL.   She knows

DRUID.   what stars to gather

DRUID.   into dancing shapes

DRUID.   of animals,

DRUID.   birds and fish,

DRUID.   creatures of the forest

(BRESAL moves forward)

BRESAL.   Gliding through the heavens,

DRUID.   she hangs the night

DRUID.   with jewelled clusters

DRUID.   of dancing constellations

BRESAL.   *(joyful)* lighting up the sky with stars

(DRUIDS move SR. and SL. facing SCREEN, with BRESAL DSR.)

DRUID.   She knows

DRUID.   Fire Queen of the Sky

FIREFLIES.   *(overlapping whisper)* Etare,Etare,Etare

DRUID.   Only She knows

BRESAL.   how to make the stars dance

(*MUSIC as LIGHTS fade up behind SCREEN US. where FIREFLIES dance holding stars (giving the effect of twinkling lights) As Screen DANCE of FIREFLIES ends, FADE MUSIC.LIGHTS change*)

DRUID.   Where is the Druid Bresal Etarlaim? Let him step forward

BRESAL.   (*comes centre stage*) I am he

DRUID.   Prove to us you deserve the name of Druid

BRESAL.   (*shocked*) Why should I?

DRUID.   (*moves nearer BRESAL*) otherwise you will be cast from this land

DRUID.   (*moves nearer BRESAL*) to roam in the wilderness all of your days

BRESAL.   For what reason?

(*A PAUSE*)

BRESAL.   (*beseeching*) I tell you I am worthy

DRUID.   Prove it

DRUID.   Tell your tale

DRUID.   Make sure it is true

DRUID.   otherwise

DRUID.   it will be the worse for you

(A PAUSE)

BRESAL.   *(tentatively)* My tale concerns Midhir and the Firefly

DRUID. *(scoffs)* What would Midhir of the Mighty Arm and High Good Looks

DRUID.   want with a firefly?

BRESAL.   Listen and I will tell you

(DRUIDS settle for the tale, seated in clusters SR.& SL.)

BRESAL.   *(glances at DRUIDS, then)* It all began with the jealousy of a woman

DRUID.   A jealous woman always brings misfortune

(DRUIDS laugh)

BRESAL.   One evening Fuamach, Wife to Midhir sent for me

(Enter FUAMACH, Wife to Midhir, black haired, spiteful)

FUAMCH.   Bresal Etarlaim find me a powerful
love potion

BRESAL.   For yourself?

FUAMACH.   Are your brains made of bran? No,
not for me

BRESAL.   Then for whom?

FUAMACH.   For Midhir of The Mighty Arm
and High Good Looks who *(heated)* fought for me
against all the Chieftains in the island

BRESAL.   So he did

FUAMACH.   Who wooed and won me with
words of love

BRESAL.   That is true

FUAMACH.   You were there when he carried me
off on the feast of Bealtaine

BRESAL.   I was

FUAMACH.   Tell me Druid, how can such a man
as that now turn his back on me?

BRESAL.   *(Sl.Pause)* No man likes a jealous woman

FUAMACH.   But I am his wife

BRESAL.   Take care you keep it so

FUAMACH.   *(goes to him)* How so -- with such bitterness in my breast and a longing that is like a sickness coming over me?

(A PAUSE)

BRESAL.   There may be no hope for you. But I will try *(pauses)*   I am going to the hazel wood.   Be patient.Wait here until I send   for   you *(turns to go, then sensing her following him,turns back)* or if you must follow keep well out of sight

(BRESAL moves around stage, followed by FUAMACH who conceals herself)

DRUID. Women want power

DRUID. on Earth

DRUID. as in the Heavens

(DRUIDS laugh)

BRESAL.   As luck would have it I chanced upon Midhir walking in the shadows of the night

(LIGHTS darker.Enter MIDHIR, strong, golden haired)

MIDHIR.   *(pacing)*   I am beset by Fuamach whose breast grows ever more full of jealousy

72

BRESAL.   *(over to him)* Leave her to me

MIDHIR.   *(sighs)*   Would I were wed to someone bright and beautiful

BRESAL.   Like a jewel shining in the night?

MIDHIR.   *(pauses)* Would it were so

BRESAL.   *(looking up)* Like the brightest star in the firmanent?

MIDHIR.   *(sighs)* If only it could be so

(A PAUSE)

BRESAL.   I know where such a one can be found

MIDHIR.   Druid, I am too weary for your jesting

BRESAL.   This is no jest

MIDHIR.   Where? Tell me where?

BRESAL.   *(extends his hand to MIDHIR)* Let me lead you there. First you must close your eyes. Where we go no man has gone   *(as MIDHIR looks at him in surprise)* Hush! Come with me

(HE binds Midhir's eyes with a cloth and leads him around stage, followed secretly by FUAMACH)

BRESAL.   So when Bear was lighting the heavens

73

BRESAL   and Orion's belt gleaming in the distance, I brought Midhir blindfold into the hazel wood. There I made a potion for him *(MIMES this, gives it to MIDHIR)* Drink this and sleep. When you awake you will fall in love with the first woman you see

(MIDHIR mimes drinking potion)

FUAMACH. *(aside)* And by all the deer of the forest that will be me

BRESAL   So away with Fuamach to make herself beautiful in her best robes for the moment when Midhir would fall in love with her

(FUAMACH hurries off)

BRESAL.   As the night grew dark I watched the Heavens and beheld the Queen of Fire counting her stars

(LIGHTS   change. He turns to faces Screen US. where twinkling lights are seen)

ALL.   She knows

BRESAL.   the shape and size of every star

ALL.   She knows

BRESAL.   who they are

DRUID.   whence they came

74

DRUID.   where they are found

ALL.   She knows

DRUID.   what stars to gather

DRUID.   into dancing shapes

DRUID.   of animals

DRUID.   birds and fish

DRUID.   creatures of the forest

(A PAUSE)

BRESAL.   As Midhir slept in the wood I watched the heavens and beheld the stars dancing and turning as the Fire Queen of the Sky

FIREFLIES. *(overlapping whisper)* Etare,Etare,Etare

BRESAL.   brought forth her stars to dance

(DRUIDS Look out front)

BRESAL.   As I watched She called every star by name and led them into the dance

(DRUIDS merge   into shadows at side of stage with BRESAL   DSR. MUSIC fades up gently as LIGHTS CHANGE & FIRE QUEEN appears on stage. As SHE calls the constellations, ETAIN & FIREFLIES dance on stage in incandescent clothes, holding twinkling lights)

FIRE QUEEN.   Orion

(Stars form shape and dance)

FIRE QUEEN. Pegasus

(Stars form shape and dance)

FIRE QUEEN. Cassiopeia

(Stars form shape and dance. As MUSIC fades, DANCERS glide off behind Screen US., now lit from behind and on which flickering lights become still. SPOT on BRESAL DSR.)

BRESAL.   The dancing stars became transfixed except for one, brighter and more sparkling than all the rest

DRUID.   The Queen of Fire, like everyone, has her favourites

BRESAL.   I could not take my gaze from it *(amazed)* Then spinning high over the trees, it danced

DRUID.   Sorcery!

(MUSIC as Black clad DANCER, waving a twinkling light, leads BRESAL a playful dance around the stage)
.

BRESAL.   Taking my wand I followed the Star - out of the hazel wood, over the hills, to the shore where at Bealtaine the Island People light fires

FIREFLIES. *(whisper overlapping)* Etare, Etare,Etare

BRESAL. With my wand I made Midhir come to where the Star danced on the shore and bade him take off the cloth that covered his eyes

(MIME .MIDHIR has moved as in a trance to BRESAL who points excitedly to Spinning Star (black clad DANCER)

BRESAL. Look I can make the stars dance!

(A Shocked silence)

DRUID.   Only She,

DRUID.   Fire Queen of the Sky

FIREFLIES.   *(whisper overlapping)* Etare, Etare,Etare

DRUID.   can make the stars dance

(BRESAL MIMES waving wand, watched by an entranced MIDHIR. A FIRE,composed of FIREFLIES, who conceal ETAIN, wearing flame coloured garments, forms SC.)

BRESAL. Again I waved my wand and behold a fire sprang up on the shore

DRUID.   The Gods of Bealtaine are not mocked

BRESAL. As I waved my wand to the left of me the Spinning Star danced into the fire *(pauses)* and when I

BRESAL   looked again in place of the Star was a Firefly

(As black clad DANCER merges into FIRE of FIREFLIES SC. then exits US.,A FIREFLY, dances, flickers in and out of FIRE)

FIREFLIES. *(whisper overlapping)* Etare, Etare,Etare

BRESAL. *(excited)* As I waved my wand around me, in a wide arc, I looked again and, before my very eyes, the Firefly became a beautiful woman *(pauses)* and Midhir was enchanted by her

(CHORD of MUSIC as ETAIN, shimmering in flame coloured garments, emerges from FIRE (composed of FIREFLIES) MIDHIR approaches ETAIN in wonder. MUSIC as THEY dance in the light of the fire. As dance ends THEY gaze at each other)

DRUID.   Sorcery!

BRESAL.   And, as darkness crept over the land, they danced in the light of the fire

DRUID.   You were the one seduced

(A PAUSE)

MIDHIR.   Who are you?

ETAIN.   They call me Etain

MIDHIR.   Etain. It is a shining name

ETAIN.   *(playful)* Does it please you?

MIDHIR.   Oh they have named you well *(mimes caressing her hair)* Your hair gleams like the colour of red gold after it is rubbed *(mimes touching her shoulders)* In the firelight there is a glowing light on your shoulders and *(mimes caressing her feet)* and, when you dance, your feet sparkle like two stars

(MUSIC as ETAIN dances. MIDHIR then takes her hand. MUSIC fades as THEY EXIT dancing)

BRESAL.   *(looking after them)* As Midhir of the Mighty Arm danced with the Firefly into the hazel wood I watched until she was no more than a glimmer in the dark cloak of the Night

(LIGHTS up as for Day. DRUIDS circle BRESAL)

ALL.   Bresal Etarlaim, who are you to desire control of the Heavens? Is the Earth not enough?

DRUID.   Have you forgotten the art of a Druid?

ALL.   The Fires at Bealtaine implore the Gods for prosperity,

DRUID.   fruitful crops for the island people

DRUID.   fertile slopes for cattle

ALL.   The art of a Druid is

DRUID.   To bring peace on Earth
.
ALL.   not control the Heavens!

(DRUIDS confer angrily)

BRESAL.   *(pleading)* Hear me out

DRUID.   Let him continue

(DRUIDS go to both sides and sit in stony silence)

BRESAL.   When Cassiopeia was high in the
Heavens, I beheld a flickering *(pauses)* Then, out of
the darkness, that covered the hazel wood, Midhir
and the Firefly came dancing towards me

*(MUSIC   as MIDHIR and ETAIN ENTER, dance SC.
smiling at each other, FUAMACH enters DSR. in her
best robes, stares horrified at ETAIN, moves to BRESAL)*

FUAMACH.   Who is that woman I see with Midhir
of the Mighty Arm?

BRESAL.   What you see is a firefly. Nothing more

FUAMACH.   By all the deer of the forest now I
know your brains are made of bran

BRESAL. *(soothing)* Fuamach,Wife to Midhir, if I
wave my wand the firefly will disappear & fly away

80

FUAMACH.   You think I will believe that?

BRESAL.   I will prove it to you

FUAMACH.   Then wave your wand and be quick about it

BRESAL.   *(mimes waving wand)* So I changed her back into a firefly

(MUSIC.ETAIN becomes Firefly, EXITS dancing. MIDHIR is confused)

BRESAL.   and Midhir of the Mighty Arm was lost without her

MIDHIR.   *(to BRESAL)* Is that a vision? *(looks after firefly)*

FUAMACH.   *(to BRESAL)* His wits are gone thanks to you

MIDHIR.   *(confused)* Am I dreaming?

FUAMACH.   *(takes his hand)* Come home and sleep *(During following speech, FUAMACH leads MIDHIR SL. Mimes giving him sleeping potion which he drinks. BOTH lie down extreme SL.)*

BRESAL.   She gave Midhir a sleeping potion to forget and made him lie by her side so he would not leave her ever *(pauses)* As he fell into a deep sleep, she thought that was the end of Midhir and the Firefly

81

(Day LIGHTS)

DRUID.   How can we believe you deserve the name of Druid?

DRUID.   First a star leads you a merry dance

BRESAL.   That is so

DRUID.   After that a firefly dances to your wand

BRESAL.   That is true

DRUID.   Then you turn the firefly into a woman

BRESA.   I tell you it is so

DRUID.   Now the woman is again a firefly

BRESAL.   That is the way of it

DRUID.   For shame!

(DRUIDS confer angrily)

BRESAL.   *(pleading)* My tale is not yet done

DRUID.   What more mischief is there?

BRESAL.   What I now tell you concerns how Midhir and the Firefly came to be in the house of Etar, King of the Sidhe

DRUID. Will you ever learn not to meddle in things

DRUID.   that are beyond you?

BRESAL.   Let me continue

(DRUIDS Exchange looks, then a DRUID nods curtly at BRESAL. LIGHTS fade up behind US. Screen where we see FIREFLY dancing restlessly. Sound of WIND)

BRESAL. While Midhir lay sleeeping ,the Firefly was blown to and fro throughout the land in great misery until one day, she came to the house of Etar, King of the Sidhe, where there was a wedding feast

(Merrymaking Sounds. DRUIDS turn towards US. SCREEN where during next speech we see:. Silhouette of chalice, Then a gleaming light (held by black clad DANCER behind Screen) dazzling down into chalice. Silhouette of Crowned Queen appears, raises chalice to mouth. Merrymaking Sounds in b/g).

BRESAL.   Dazzled by the gleam of the goblet in the hand of Etar's bride,the Firefly fell from a beam in the roof down into the goblet and, as Etar's bride raised it to her lips, the Firefly was drunk along with the wine and swallowed

(LIGHTS change)

DRUID.   See what mischief you have caused with your meddling

DRUID. The art of the Druid is to hold the Earth in balance

DRUID.   Wisdom,

DRUID.   To keep the peace

DRUID.   Harmony

DRUIDS.   To heal, nourish and obey

DRUID.   Not to meddle in things that do not concern you

DRUIDS.   Have you learnt nothing from us?

BRESAL.   Hear me out

(DRUIDS confer)

DRUID.   Let him continue

(A CHORD OF MUSIC)

BRESAL.   While Midhir of the Mighty Arm lay sleeping, Etain was born again and grew into a beautiful woman

ALL DRUIDS.   Why did you meddle with the Firefly? Why could you not leave her as she was, nothing more than a flicker in the dark cloak of the Night?

(LIGHTS change)

BRESAL.   And, when King Eochaid caught sight of Etain he was enchanted and wanted her for himself

(ENTER KING EOCHAID and ETAIN, who join hands)

BRESAL.   So he marries Etain, daughter of Etar,
King of the Sidhe, and it is their grandson, Conaire,
that will be High King of Ireland

*(MUSIC as COURTIERS, WARRIORS,WOMEN enter,
robed for Wedding Feast. THEY mingle, flirt etc. during
following. MEN admire ETAIN, envy KING EOCHAID)*

BRESAL.   And, hearing music, Midhir awoke and
came to the place of the wedding feast. And he looked
on Etain, full of love for her, watching as she dazzled
all who caught sight of her loveliness

*(During above speech, MIDHIR rises, moves SC., watches
DANCERS. FUAMACH   stirs, searches in vain for
MIDHIR, runs offstage L. MIDHIR lures ETAIN DSR.)*

MIDHIR.   Do you not know me?

ETAIN.   *(hesitates)* I am not sure.

MIDHIR.   Before this day you danced with me

ETAIN.   *(surprised)* Tell me

MIDHIR.   By the light of the fire that night on
the shore and after in the hazel wood

ETAIN.   *(looks confused, then takes his hand)* Then,
dance now at my wedding feast

(MIDHIR and ETAIN join DANCERS SC.)

BRESAL.   She led him into her wedding dance and while she danced, she gave such a look of longing towards Midhir of the Mighty Arm that his heart was almost torn from his breast and he vowed to win her back

(MIDHIR lures her DS. of DANCERS)

MIDHIR.   Before he laid eyes on you, you were mine

ETAIN.   *(looks at him)* I know now this is true but *(looks towards KING EIOCHAID)* I am married to the King

MIDHIR.   Then I will challenge the King for your hand

ETAIN.   *(gazes at him)* And I will go with you if he gives me leave

(KING claims ETAIN as partner. SHE dances, torn between MIDHIR & KING. As MUSIC fades, DANCERS EXIT. LIGHTS change)

BRESAL.   And taking his spear and shield, Midhir set out toward the hill near the hazel wood

(MIDHIR in Mime takes spear & shield, moves around stage, stops when HE approaches KING EOCHAID)

MIDHIR.   King Eochaid, I challenge you

KING.   To what end?

MIDHIR.   Let us fight before I answer that

KING.   So be it

BRESAL.   *(To DRUIDS)* And a hard fight it was

(THEY fight. KING EOCHAID falls)

KING.   *(breathless)* I am beaten *(rises helped by MIDHIR)* What is your reward?

MIDHIR.   I claim Etain, daughter of Etar

KING. *(horrified)* My bride? No!

MIDHIR.   Where is your honour as a King?

(A PAUSE)

KING. Let us fight again

MIDHIR.   This time the reward will be Etain

KING.   *(reluctant)* So be it

BRESAL.   And, with a mighty roar King Eochaid fell upon Midhir of the Mighty Arm

(THEY fight)

BRESAL.   And Midhir was ready to hit back when the voice of a woman called out

(FUAMACH enters agitated)

FUAMACH. I will find him if it is the last thing I do. I swear by all the deer of the forest *(horrified)* Do not harm a hair of his head *(shouts)* Make them halt for Pity's sake!

BRESAL. And,as Fuamach, Wife to Midhir flung herself between the warriors, she prevented the King's spear piercing the heart of Midhir, but was wounded herself

(FUAMACH rushes between them, is wounded and carried off)

BRESAL. And so she was carried off, still full of love for Midhir of the Mighty Arm. And he, with a shout, leaped upon the King

(THEY fight)

BRESAl. And Midhir of the Mighty Arm overcame King Eochaid

(ETAIN runs in upset, weeps & stands beside MIDHIR)

KING. Where are my warriors?

(WARRIORS rush in and try to attack MIDHIR)

ETAIN. *(glances upwards,whispers pleadingly)* Etare! Etare Etare! There is no one who does not fear The Fire Queen of the Sky - even the Druids *(pauses, intense whisper)* Etare,Etare, Etare!

BRESAl.   As the King's warriors came to his aid,The
Fire Queen of the Sky sent a storm of falling stars

(Black clad DANCERS   waving twinkling lights dazzle
WARRIORS in hand to hand combat. KING and
WARRIORS are defeated)

BRESAL.   and the King's men were dazzled by the
falling stars   sent by the Fire Queen of the sky

(MIDHIR and ETAIN move US. towards Screen)

BRESAl.   Midhir of the Mighty Arm seized Etain
and off with them up through the roof of the house

(FIREFLIES gather around ETAIN and MIDHIR. FIRE
QUEEN enters)

BRESAL.   Then, the Fire Queen came in her chariot
and took Etain up with her into the starry sky to find
a place for her and a place for Midhir beside her so
that, joined together they can sparkle and shine like
the brightest jewels in the necklace of the dark sky of
the Night *(moves to stand DSR.)*

(MUSIC. FIRE   QUEEN leads MIDHIR and ETAIN,
(who are   given   twinkling lights) in a dance   with
FIREFLIES. PAUSE. LIGHTS change)

ALL.   Bresal Etarlaim, your wits are crazed with all
this stargazing.Go & do the bidding of the Fire Queen

DRUID.   who heals the hole in the sky caused by

DRUID.   your havoc

DRUID.   while we keep the balance here on Earth

(TWO DRUIDS step forward)

ALL.   Go now and do not return until She has restored harmony in the Heavens

DRUID. Till then you will be seen, spinning and dancing like a falling star

DRUID.   All over the heavens, never finding rest until She, Fire Queen of the Sky

FIREFLIES. *(overlapping whisper)* Etare, Etare, Etare

ALL.   makes you her own
.
(THREE DRUIDS step forward)

ALL.   changing your shape into a creature of the forest

DRUID   to join a constellation if she so wishes

(ALL DRUIDS step forward)

ALL.   And the name of Bresal Etarlaim lives only in this story

(DRUIDS banish BRESAL ETARLAIM US. FIRE QUEEN indicates that he go behind US. Screen. HE

obeys. DRUIDS face out front)

ALL.   He must learn that only She, Fire Queen of the
Sky

FIREFLIES. *(whisper overlapping)* Etare, Etare, Etare

ALL.   Can make the stars dance

*(DRUIDS exit SR.& SL. MUSIC. LIGHTS change as
FIRE QUEEN gathers Stars into a dance around MIDHIR
& ETAIN. Fade to BLACKOUT. In BLACKOUT, Stars
(twinkling lights held by DANCERS) dance as MUSIC
fades)*

(END OF PLAY)